Triumphal scene

(from *Aida*)

Text by Antonio Ghislanzoni
English translation: John Rutter

cresc. e string. a poco a poco

OXFORD UNIVERSITY PRESS MUSIC DEPARTMENT
WALTON STREET, OXFORD OX2 6DP · 198 MADISON AVENUE, NEW YORK, NY 10016

4

6

8

14

-ro - - - - i, i lau - ri, i fior ver - siam!
na - - - - tion, laurels and flowers we bring!

ro - - i,
na - - tion,

-ro - - - - i,
na - - - - tion,

il guar-do er-ge - - te;
of - fer your hum - ble thanks;

pesante

H Più animato (♩ = 132)

mf

CHORUS OF PRIESTS

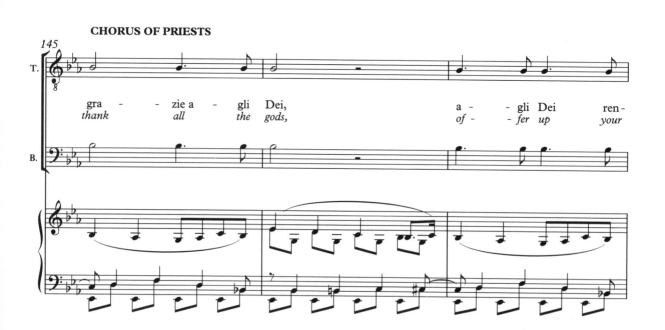

T.

gra - - zie a - gli Dei, a - - gli Dei ren-
thank all the gods, of - - fer up your

B.

162
-rier, vie - ni a gio-ir con no - i, sul pas - so de - gli e
praise, ho - nour and sa - lu - ta - tion, O he - roes of our
ff
gra - zie a-gli Dei,
thanks to the gods,
ff
166
-ro - i i lau - rie i fior ver-siam. Vie - ni o guer -
na - tion, flow'rs and lau - rels we bring. Hail, migh - ty
gra - zie a - gli Dei,
thanks to all the gods,

20

22

Printed and bound in Great Britain by
Caligraving Limited Thetford Norfolk

The Oxford Choral Classics
Octavo Series

*A unique library of the shorter choral classics
in authoritative, practical, and attractively priced editions*

Edited by JOHN RUTTER

The Oxford Choral Classics Octavo Series makes the best new editions of standard repertoire available to every choir at an attractive price.

Drawing on his extensive experience of the needs of choirs and their directors, John Rutter has compiled a comprehensive selection of shorter choral masterpieces from the Renaissance to the twentieth century. The series comprises a variety of both secular and sacred music, including madrigals, part-songs, opera choruses, sacred choruses, motets, anthems, and Christmas music.

Every piece has been hand-picked for its musical quality and attractiveness, newly edited from the most reliable sources (eliminating many long-standing errors), and engraved and printed to the highest Oxford standards. John Rutter's informative introductory notes place each piece in its historical context and provide useful material for programme notes.

All texts are given in their original language, with idiomatic new singing translations provided where appropriate. Unaccompanied pieces are shown with keyboard reductions, and new, playable piano accompaniments have been prepared for all orchestrally accompanied items. Clear, accurate scores and parts for the latter are available on rental from the publisher.

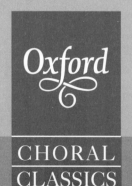

ISBN 0-19-341775-8

9 780193 417755 >